Of Darkness and Light

Of Darkness and Light

By
Fritz O'Skennick

ISBN 978-1-4461-7021-2

Dedicated to Shaun and Romana

With a big thank you to

Fire Crystal..................(New York, USA)
Janice Arndt...................(Florida, USA)
Elizabeth Anne Winter......(Kansas, USA)
Margaret Boon........(Bulawayo, Zimbabwe)
Lilly Wolf.........................(Germany)
Leesey Smuland Clark.............(VA, USA)
James Owens..................(Missouri, USA)
Kelly L.B.....................(New York, USA)
Avery Jones.....................(Texas, USA)
Helen Dunn..................(Yorkshire, UK)
Becky Blake..................(Yorkshire, UK)

For all your wonderful contributions to
the collaborations in this book and for
hours of fun playing poetry tag...
Thank you all so much, without you this
book wouldn't be possible... ☺
Xxx

Contents

Foreword

"Of Darkness and Light" is a collection of poetry and prose by Fritz O'Skennick.
"On the Fritz (Rhyme)" features new work, written in the unique style & flawless rhyme schemes that many have come to expect from his work and features many themes & genres…

"On the Fritz (Freeverse) features new work that is both powerful & thought provoking in its profound depth & unique stylings…

"Fritz & Friends" is a chapter of outstanding collaborative works with fellow poets from all over the World, including a collaboration that features no less than 40 poets in 1 poem as orchestrated and edited by Fritz via the group 'Speak to me' on the poetry site 'Allpoetry.com'

Fritz O'Skennick is an accomplished creative artist and writer with many strings to his bow. As a singer/songwriter, novelist, playwright/actor & performance poet, he has enjoyed varying successes with a number of his projects.

Previously published, some of his lighter work has appeared in various anthologies with other poets as produced by United Press. His solo debut into literary publication was **"Touching the Darkness"** a highly anticipated anthology of his dark poetry that concentrates solely on his darker work that many have come to enjoy via Allpoetry.com and via performances throughout Wales and parts of England.

His second book **"Fear the Reaper"** is a unique, intense, first-person psychological crime thriller that tells a schizophrenic tale of love, loss, revenge and madness.

This was quickly followed by his third book **"The Darkness Verses The Light"** which is a mixed genre collection of poetry, prose and short stories.

His fourth book **"Who is John Doe?"** is a unique supernatural drama based on his popular stage show of the same name.

His debut album **"UNspokeN"** (music) was released on Petrified Records in 2005 amidst a string of impressive reviews and radio play all over the world.

Playwright and acting credits include **"It could Happen to You"** and **"Who is John Doe?"** as produced by the former theatre company "Progress Cymru".

He is presently working on a second album of his music, his new book **"Just the Lyrics"** and writing his new horror novel **"Dark Confessions"**.

For further details of his poetry go to
http://allpoetry.com/Fritz%20O%20skennick

For further details of his music go to
http://www.myspace.com/fracturedpersona

For further details of his performance poetry go to
http://www.myspace.com/fritzo39skennick

On the Fritz...
-Rhyme-

Dark Alphabettie Skettie: Acrostic Alphabet...

And so I see as time has passed
Beyond the veil of hope
Clawing from the depths within
Defined by how I cope
Effervescent thoughts disperse
For life beholds the dreams
Growing from so deep within
How swift it always seems
Isolated from a world
Just loosely holding on
Knowing that the time will come
Let go the world that's gone
May I find the peace I seek
No more the raging voices
On the bough of fractured thoughts
Prevailing all my choices
Quake beneath the lonely nights
Raging mind be still
So my soul cries out its pain
To break the Demon's will
Understand and know my heart
Valor fades so far
Waking hours, full of fear with
Xylographic scars
Yield before a broken mind
Zymotic thoughts bizarre

Lost in Fictions...

Whispers in the quiet time
where shadows dance and play.
Lost to dreams and thoughts sublime
throughout the night and day.

The fatal flaw that is my bane,
no limit can I see.
I need to write to keep me sane,
and set these feelings free.

Creating fictions in my mind,
within, so dark and deep.
Curious to all I find,
that stops me finding sleep.

That I should find finality,
to ease the pain of being.
To breath my own reality,
a flicker of foreseeing.

Beneath the rays of rising dawn,
bequeathed that dreams may borrow.
A daylight lullaby is born,
that soothes in our tomorrow.

Shifting skies of lavender,
that bathe my tired mind.
Enthralled, behold its splendor
the dark and light entwined.

For now I write by candle light,
Immortal dreams are penned.
Before I find eternal night
and darkness without end.

The Paths within my Mind...

You've asked me to unlock the door
to let you peek inside,
to show you things that lie beneath,
the secrets that I hide.
And as you've asked so nicely,
I'll guide you through my mind,
but be aware I've warned you of
the dark things you may find.

The voices call beyond the void,
the darkness seeping in,
I struggle with the Demon's will
that leads my soul to sin.
I see things in the twilight time
that draws the madness near,
the ghosts that walk peripheral,
beheld but never clear.

The visions in the dream time
become my latent curse,
that speak confusion to my eyes
to scribe fatidic verse.
The whispers in the silence
that laugh and call my name,
the shifting of reality
that sets my mind aflame.

Loneliness becomes my fate,
for none can understand
a schizophrenic's heart and soul
that rests within fate's hand.
The paths that fork and fracture thoughts
that make illusions blind.
Darkness shrouds the mindscape's sight
within my broken mind.

Numbness creeping through my hopes,
consuming all my dreams,
forever walking through this life
that's never what it seems.
Creating worlds inside my mind
while loosely holding on,
my biggest fear is when I die,
this world will soon be gone.

Insomniatic Lullabies…

I've always had this problem,
I can't switch off my mind,
it stops me sleeping through the nights,
with all my thoughts combined.
Insomnia becomes my curse,
that drains me of my sleep,
whispers in the silence
that stop me counting sheep.

Visions in the darkness
building in my head,
voices calling me to scribe
their words so softly said,
begging me to tell their tales
and all they need to say
to make me see beyond the veil
in dreams beyond today.

Sleep becomes an issue,
in tricks before my eyes,
seeing worlds beyond my own,
revealing this one's lies.
Seeing passed the surface mask
that hides the deeper truth,
creation starts within the thoughts
that many lose in youth.

I wish that I could switch it off,
be normal for a while
to feel the things that humans feel
and things that make them smile.
Instead my life is so surreal,
I'm lost inside my head,
living in so many worlds
in fictions softly bled.

When I think of writer's block,
to me its just a dream,
something to aspire too
so life's not so extreme.
Go to sleep with clear thoughts,
with dreams where they should be
inside my head but when I wake,
I find that I'm still me…

Building Castles on the Moon...

If I could write a thousand years,
that speaks to you my heart.
Holding back so many tears,
bestowed now we're apart.
I'm walking in the darkness now,
no more your guiding light.
My soul befalls the starkest bough,
a path that leads to night.

So broken in the eventide,
a sun that shines its last.
A numbness creeping up inside,
that's clinging to the past.
Finding strength to carry on,
existing through the days.
Supernova soul foregone
that's burning out its blaze.

I'd give my life to see you smile,
or hold you in my arms.
Just to hear you laugh a while,
Bespelled in all your charms.
Just to hear you call my name
and reach to feel you there.
Broken hearts that beat the same,
a world apart we bare.

For now we walk in friendship's hand,
I know I must let go.
Spread your wings and fly so grand,
but know I love you so.
Life is short and passes by,
rebirth can come so soon.
To find our love won't ever die,
build castles on the moon.

Think of me and write my name,
so bold in crescent sand.
And know for you I feel the same,
so cursed by what fate's planned.
You know I'm here without you love,
you're with me in my dreams.
And as I gaze the stars above,
my heart's torn to extremes.

A Man called Fritz...

Hi there all, my name is Fritz,
My page on here gets lots of hits
My work on here so gladly fits
With all the comments that you blitz

So know I love you all to bits
From near and far and fellow Brits
Your words so kind, your awesome wits
I'm here as long as time permits

Returning comments time commits
Much more than one and all admits
Its worth it so my guilt acquits
Despite the drama, games and glitz

But lately life has been the pits
Some friends of mine, a bunch of tits
They tripped me up, I did the splits
Which wasn't good, I had the shits

An evil smell that fast emits
That travels far like it transmits
Retching, groans and coughs and spits
A crowd that drops and weakly sits

In shame I left with no omits
So red of face as shame befits
Obsess the moment bowel quits
And curse deposits it submits

So to bathroom's benefits
Stocked up with nappy changing kits
I cleaned myself, my eyes like slits
Composed myself and popped my zits

Worst of all, I'm at the Ritz
'Enough' you say of vulgar skits
And so I scribe it for my lits
Thanks for reading, your friend, Fritz

Spicing up the Sex life:
The Week of Hell...

She said our sex life was mundane
and had become routine
so we should spice it up a bit
indulge in the obscene
So I figured what the Hell?
Lets give it a go,
it should be fun to mix it up,
rekindle passion's flow.

Monday we tried dressing up,
I donned a Batman suit
and she Catwoman to my Bat,
we'd thought we'd have a hoot.
I leapt from wardrobe to the light
and swung to hear the crack,
the ceiling caved around us both
and I threw out my back.

Tuesday we tried role-play,
I met her in a bar,
the gangster and the hooker
we messed round in the car.
A tap upon the window's glass,
a frowning, outraged cop
who booked us for soliciting
because we wouldn't stop.

Wednesday I surprised her
by leaping in the room
naked as my boner sprang
'She'll like this' I assume
'GERONIMO!!!' I called out loud
and then began to choke,
her mum and gran were sitting there,
her gran then had a stroke.

Thursday we got kinky,
I chained her to the bed,
aroused to see her naked form
and naughty words she said.
a banging on the door revealed
her angry, ranting dad
who called to speak of yesterday
but saw her then went mad.

Friday, naked she sat on
my back atop a saddle
she spanked my arse coz in each hand,
she swung a ping-pong paddle
She rode me round til I was sore,
through all the rooms and halls,
til I collapsed when one mis-swing
had caught me in the balls.

Saturday we calmed it down,
massage with scented oils
to help relieve this week of hell
and all it's sex game toils,
til I felt something part my arse,
was not a nice surprise
"Vibrating Dildo 5000"
brought tears to my eyes.
I bit down on the pillow hard,
not much that I could say,
I clawed the plaster from the walls,
a bid to get away.

By Sunday, I had had enough,
and told her 'Please, no more...
I miss mundane, I like routine,
just like it was before...
No more costumes, chains or spanks,
or objects in my arse,
no more surprises you have planned,
or schemes you must surpass.'
'Fine' she said 'I'll call my friend
and cancel our three-way'
I looked at her through narrowed eyes,
my jaw dropped in dismay.
'Don't be hasty by my words'
I grinned and calmly tried
'Good, coz Bernard's on his way'
she said and so I cried...

...And cried... And cried...

Mankind: A Working Progress...

So many things throughout our world,
so much that we've forgot.
Like things declared impossible,
until its proved they're not.
Progress comes in many forms,
necessity its muse.
For every gift that's dreamt by man,
within this world we use.

Homer said the world was flat
and all believed his word.
That ships would fall off from its edge,
'til it was proved absurd.
Columbus charged with Heresy,
until his sails unfurled.
And proved we live upon a globe
and showed a bigger World.

They said that man would never fly
and scorned Da Vinci's dream.
And ridiculed attempts he made
in thoughts that seemed extreme.
It showed he dreamed beyond his years
Wright Brothers made their flights
A monumental day for Man,
like birds we soar to heights.

Newton showed us gravity,
and Edison, the light,
Franklin tamed the lightning's wrath,
such dreams as they ignite.
Graham Bell bestowed the phone,
and artists speak their dreams.
Music, art and literature
and movies now it seems.

They said we'd never reach the moon,
too grand a dream to do.
That we could never touch the stars
'til dreamer's dreams came true.
A giant leap for all Mankind,
with naught we can't achieve.
If only we could live in peace
and trust we could believe.

Of all the gifts bestowed to us
through ages way back when,
the one that means the most to me
would have to be my pen.
It grants me means to scribe my words
and share with you my heart.
It lets me show you what's inside,
the muse that writes my art.

So look into your mirror's gaze,
be proud of what you are.
You're from a race that's growing up,
who's dreams can reach so far.
So when you laugh and ridicule
and scorn a wacky scheme.
Remember fools who laughed before
and scorned the dreamers dream.

For only with the sight to dream
can you see what's to come.
So much that we have yet to do
in dreams bestowed to some.
Think of all we have achieved,
for doubts there are a lot.
'coz all is deemed impossible
until its proved its not…

On the Fritz…
-Freeverse-

And so I Scream...

The Demon cries out,
banishing me
to the darkness,
his breath like frost
upon my heart,
his touch becomes
an eclipse
upon my soul...

So creative is he,
so artistic
in his games
as he begins
to ravish my mind,
leaving me deranged
and barely lucid...

The dreamscapes
he'll paint,
such lipstick lusts
lost in
groggy thoughts,
to fawn upon
my ethereal desires,
tainting them,
making them gritty,
livid in their fading...

...and so I scream...

Facets...

The master poet,
so full of passion,
strength and desire,
bearing his soul
to the world
in profound rhapsodies
bestowed by his love
of the written word…

The damaged musician,
riddled with insecurity,
expressing his heart
in a plethora
of melodies
that haunt,
taunt and rage
in a distortion
of whimsical clarity…

The prolific writer,
creating worlds
and giving life
to the souls
who'll live there,
a God who decrees
every action
but allows his creations
enough free will
to guide the plots
that bind them
to his imagination…

The eccentric actor,
a chameleon
bringing life
to the words
of the writer,
striving for credibility
in the masks
that he'll wear
to the watchers
of his beloved craft...

The egotistical performer,
a visible sentience
to the poet
and the musician,
expressing their art
with a passion
that reflects the soul
of the actor
yet differs
in translations
of changing continuity...

The lonely schizophrenic,
bounced around
the mental health system,
desperately trying
to be whole
amidst an army of voices
and delusional states
that plague his fragile,
fragmented mind,
but he fights his demons
to hold a truce of reason
to live another day…

The wary psychic,
sensitive to the ripples
and cracks in reality,
lost to visions
that are as prophetic
as they are misleading
as the eidolon
breach the bough
of the quiet time,
each so desperately
wanting to be heard
on a path between
the darkness and the light…

The doting father,
the dutiful son,
the sibling rivalry,
the best friend,
each rejecting
the role
of the
fading lover,
sacrificed
that the others
may thrive without
the complexities
of distraction
and hormonal cravings
that burden the mind,
crush the soul
and break the heart…

A fractured persona,
living so many lives,
wearing so many masks
that conflict
in the choices made,
defining the boundaries
in the facets
of all that he perceives,
all that he was,
all that he is
and one day
all that he will become…

And so he seeks salvation
in the alignment
that will
make him
whole,
holding
the
hope
that
one
day…

…he'll be a real boy…

Alphabetic Truths...

Anomalies Beheld,
Causality Devastated,
Effervescent Futurities
Growing Haunted
In Jaundiced Knowledge,
Left Metaphorically Numb,
Often Pulped, Quantified,
Rectified, Savagely Torn
Under Vagaries
Wrought Xenomorphic...

...Yesterday's Zenith...

Each word begins with the next letter of the Alphabet

The Oncoming Storm...

Beware the oncoming storm,
static charging RAGE
as electric tendril fingers
caress the TURBULENT cerebrum,
a CRY that rolls like thunder
to the tears of a TROUBLED sky,
torrential in its outpouring
from a DARKLING cloud,
burst from a TAUT
medulla oblongata,
such PAIN
as lightning cracks,
a bellow of devastation,
PULSE beating
through temples,
drumming
beneath fingertips
as FIRE ignites
swiftly behind
RED rimmed eyes
that struggle
to hold back a FURY,
so long repressed
in the decaying psyche
of a BROKEN mind...

...Ground Zero for the coming VOLCANO day...

In the Name of Vanity...

Flesh replaced by steel,
more than a theory,
less than a saving grace,
an imitation of life
to chisel away
the imperfections of man...

For the mirror lies,
hazardous in the
perceptions of vanity.
The dandelion,
although one man's weed,
becomes another man's flower...

And so continues a famine
of the soul as natural beauty
is lost in insecurities
committed in
atrocities of the flesh...

The tapestry of life sings
a mournful lullaby,
unraveled in the eyes of fate
beheld in a din of chaos
as worlds collide
and hope is lost...

So slippery is the path that we walk,
reality usurped by fantasy,
casting shadows of darkness
over a doomed humanity,
becoming a chameleon
to dreams of the lives we crave…

A looming deadline approaches,
an end to perceptions of self,
lost to the cry of voices
that boom and shout
in outrage and warning…

We are throwing our children
to the wolves,
burying them in shallow lives,
teaching them
to worship the superficial
in the name of perfection…

And so they will judge
and be judged on guise,
never looking beyond the surface
to the beauty within,
forever wondering why
they can't wipe the dirt
from their hands
nor find a truth
that is constant
nor a happiness
that lasts beyond the moment…

The darkness is coming and we are the bringers…

Llenoy Bkreon Hraet...

Lsot wihitn dptehs
of draksens
taht cnilg, calw and taer
at my suol,
rppiing itno my hraet,
fcanig tutrhs
bteetr lfet brueid
in cnotpmet
of fdanig psasoins
taht lvaee me nugaht
but pian and sroorw...

How lnog msut I ednrue
tihs nbmuesns of bineg?
Why msut it awlyas
end lkie tihs?
Am I rlaely dsetneid
to fcae lfie aonle?
Need bcoeems ncessetiy,
lgnonig, my yraneed upitoa,
taht I may fnid
scuh lvoe as I
so dapesterley seek...

A psiorn of my own mkanig,
blidunig me up to flal,
awlyas lavenig
me etpmy of hpoe,
hlloow of felenig
tuohgrhuot my suol's
iennr ternomt,
cganig my hraet
to all taht wulod
psurue it's lvoe...

Aals my hraet has bkreon
too mnay tmies,
inorgnig sgins
taht fezere
my suol to sonte,
rjeetcnig all
taht seek aeittotnns
of its msot craanl dsriees
as ralaeiztoin dwans
in an ehppinay
taht skahes the fdnuotaoins
of my vrey bineg…

…It is not to be…

Lonely Broken Heart...

Lost within depths
of darkness
that cling, claw and tear
at my soul,
ripping into my heart,
facing truths
better left buried
in contempt
of fading passions
that leave me naught
but pain and sorrow...

How long must I endure
this numbness of being?
Why must it always
end like this?
Am I really destined
to face life alone?
Need becomes necessity,
longing, my yearned utopia,
that I may find
such love as I
so desperately seek...

A prison of my own making,
building me up to fall,
always leaving
me empty of hope,
hollow of feeling
throughout my soul's
inner torment,
caging my heart
to all that would
pursue its love...

Alas my heart has broken
too many times,
ignoring signs
that freeze
my soul to stone,
rejecting all
that seek attentions
of its most carnal desires
as realization dawns
in an epiphany
that shakes the foundations
of my very being…

…It is not to be…

Drained...

...Drained...
...Lifeless... Numb...

Lost beyond the
dark perceptions
of physicality,
locked in a repetition
of troubled thoughts
that plague
and torment
in a storm
of obsessive turmoil...

Clawing from the depths,
raging to a fury unspent,
burned in a fire of truth
that shatters
illusion's comfort,
bursting the bubble
of hope
that held chimera dreams
so safe for so very long...

...Drained...
...Hollow... Empty...

Exposed beyond humility,
a shell that once held
such life and love
in such fervent ardor,
lays waste
in the purgatory
of paramnesia's waltz,
forsaken in the eyes
of vociferous solitude...

Like sand seeping
through a
fractured hour glass,
time loses its
linear chronology
as the dawning rays
of aurora's glare
gently warm
barren sightless eyes,
lost to the thrall
of phrenetic
night whispers...

...Tearless... Obtund...
...Drained...

The Beginning of the End...

So suddenly the storm breaks...
With such disdain, the voices rage
as crimson tears fall,
so pure against the stark scream
of a broken mind,
finding belonging
in a tide of shattered dreams,
choking on the ashes of promise,
an end that feels so near
but never comes...

Emphatic whispers in the silence
as hate bubbles below the surface,
obsessing trivialities
that call for revenge
on those that trespass against us,
hollow apologies that
appease the guilty hearts,
too little, too late,
crying in the solitude,
for empty words are never enough...

Chaos bleeds from the scars of emotion,
unseen to the eye,
oblivious to the dying soul,
cutting so deep inside,
evolved by compulsions
that become absolute,
a mistake to be made over and over
and so fingertips gently caress
the revolver's cold metal surface,
drawing it toward me...

Life is a privilege to those
with the courage to stay and live it,
but that is not me…
I am so alone,
each day I disguise my thoughts
behind a pompous smile
as my mind crumbles a little more,
blurring the boundary of reality,
breaking my will to fight
before an inquisition of pain…

The way out is obvious, even to me…
It is the beginning of the end,
such grave thoughts
in the midnight of my soul,
my body covered
in an abundance of fading scars
like a map that draws a path
that swiftly leads me here…
to this moment… this place… this hour…

pushing the barrel up under my chin,
I close my eyes
and………………………

Sibylline Whispers...

Transcendental dreamscapes
ascending the veneer
of perceived actuality,
darkness bleeding
through CRACKS
in the entropy,
eroding the EDGES
of reality...

...Losing TIME...

...Losing SELF...

...Temporal chronology
NO longer linear...

Its nature vacillates,
mutating in ATROPHY,
as memories ally
to delphian DREAMS
as the PATH splits in twain,
then thrice fractured
to pythonic whispers
that FILL the VOID
in visions
that resound and SCREAM
in a MAELSTROM of voices,
HOWLING in a storm of RAGE,
LOST on the WINDS of change
with DIVINE revelations
that are as judicious
as they ARE infelicitous...

The barrier IS failing,
breaking down
as realities BLEED,
merge and weave,
rethreading the tapestry,
HOLDING existence
in the BALANCE,
boldly rising
from the DARK time,
an ECHO of
the forgotten genesis,
rewriting the slate,
UNSEEN, unfelt, unknown
by ALL but those
touched by MADNESS,
BROKEN prophets,
beheld in the EYES
of SUBLIME chaos…

Perceiving the FACES
that GLIMPSE
through the VEIL,
KNOWING untold
of the caller's CHIME,
finding AXIOM
in a STRANGER'S projection,
ATTUNED to the shadows
of restless EIDOLON,
a MADNESS of sanity,
a SHARD of truth,
cocooned in a LIE,
WRAPPED in a blind
psychic psychosis
that FINDS life
in a fragmented MIND
that SEES all…

…Yet STRUGGLES to be WHOLE…

Thin Ice...

Do not
presume
to know
that what
I see
is not real
because
it is not
tangible
to your
eyes

Do not
think
that what
I hear
is a lie
perceived
by my
fears
in a
chorus
of voices
in an
orchestra
of
madness

You skate
on the ice
of causality,
never
looking
below,
embracing a
superficial
surface
on a lake
of
perception,
oblivious
to the
depths
that stir
beneath
your
feet

I see
your cold,
sterile
world
above me
through
the algid
crystal
window,
frosted
in a
distortion of
two
dimensional
reality,
reflected
in the
cracks
that form
at the
edges of
entropic
physicality

The irony
that you
believe me
beneath
you
is not
lost on me,
for
though
I am born
of the
light,
I was cast
to the
darkness,
lost to
the
madness,
to speak
its voice
through a
looking
glass
of
fractured
quintessence

And so
I wait
as visions
come
to pass,
staving
a path
twixt
the shadows
of
uncertainty,
beheld
in the tears
of the
Angels
lament
in a fortress
of shattered
dreams,
honed through
the sagacity
of a
broken
psyche,
beyond
the empty
lives
that skate
above
the thin ice

And so, one by one…

…they will fall…

Atrum Oraculum…

Beware the coming storm,
the thriving atrophy
that draws ever closer,
growing from the shadows
of time's entropic decay…

The evolving darkness
consumes the fading light
in a divine reckoning
that snuffs the flame
of perception's falsehoods…

The time is almost upon us,
we must prepare the way,
as we behold the shift
of anomalous futurities,
that all may find confluence
in the coming days…

For madness shall find sanity
in evolution of perception,
as sanity finds confusion
in its devout inability
to accept the veil's falling…

And so the walls
will come tumbling down
as rationality lies obsolete
in an extinction of life
as we know it,
adrift on a tide
of fear and confusion
befallen on a lost humanity…

We have strayed from the path,
deceived in an age of reason
that is not what it decrees,
creating a cold,
sterile world
of greed and
impurity justified
in the guise of progress…

And so the nature of man
shall be revealed,
forsaken in the flames
of hypocrisy,
unravelled
as the tapestry burns,
sculpting life
from the ashes
of the past
to build castles
from the stones of change…

…The catalyst of vicissitude is upon us...

…Caveo Obscurum...

Paradoxal Pariah...

I walk in the breach
between worlds,
a worn path of
endless potentialities,
fragile in its instability
to change its nature,
beset by darkness
in mood swings
so destructive
as to burn
the stars
from the skies
as the agents
of chaos
dance
in the fires
of paradox,
feeding
on the ashes
of causality,
distorting
the balance,
rewriting
the pages
of eternity

from
the blood
of the
forgotten,
ceased
in the
wounds
of temporal flux,
a rip, a fold, a tear
in the fabric of reality,
bleeding new tomorrows,
spawned in illusions of today
in a fabrication of our yesterdays
that grow evermore impossible
to grasp in the shadows
of shifting actuality…

Give me
something
real
to
hold
onto…

…Please…

Evanescent Certainties...

I looked into the heart
of infinite darkness
and embraced
its sublime essence
as my own...

I gazed into the jaws
of eternity,
standing
on the threshold
of forever,
beheld in the glimmer
of the first thought
and watched
as the stars
burned
from the skies...

I have walked with Gods,
I have sung with Angels
and I have fought
with Demons,
dancing
with the Immortals
through Athanasia's
Twilight ballet...

But alas, all must
come to pass,
I have seen too much,
held too little,
I have lost so much
to the winds of time,
exhaled to dust
in a symphony of decay....

I was the Lord and Master
of Darkness,
I was the anointed Prince
of fictions,
I was the Keeper
of the Word
and I was the Bringer
of the storm...

I am a God,
bound in flesh,
a penance
of mortal frailty
that I may find humility
for my lack of compassion,
but this realisation
awakens such
pythonic anemnesis
that has lain dormant
for so very long...

Humanity is beneath me,
how can I feel clemency
when all about me,
they run rampant
like wayward children
in displays of cruelty,
greed and intolerance?
Betrayal is in their nature
and they will bring
their own destruction,
such disappointment
as they bring to me...

So much potential
evinced by so very few,
they poison me
with such
primitive emotions,
such affectivity
as I must purge
from my umbra
that it shames me
to wear their flesh,
the stink of humanity
seeping from my pores,
tainting my supreme
quintessence
in mockery
of my Godhood...

I can't live like this,
I'm fading away,
lost in the shadows
of my past,
my mind, too full,
as reality drifts
ever further
from my grasp,
memories replaced
by fictions
that are layered
and grafted
upon changing
perceptions,
building worlds
in the devastation
of time,
fulfilling a purpose
that strips me
of my acumen
til all I see
are abundant visions
so bold in their clarity
yet they distort faster
than I can scribe...

...Have I not suffered enough?

…Wraith…

…Thump, thump…
…Thump, thump…

…Heartbeat slowing…

…No, no, no…
…It cannot end like this…
…I have so much more to do…

…Thump, thump…
…Thump, thump…

…Pulse weak…

…So very cold…
…I don't want to go…
…I WILL NOT GO…

…Thump, thump…
…Thump, thump…

…Numbing cramps…

…ARRRRGH…
…Damn it, do you hear me???
…I… WILL… NOT… GO…

…Thump, thump…
…Thump…

…Clenched teeth…

…Holding on…
…Mind over matter…
…WILL RESOLUTE…

…Thump, thump…

…Light fading…

…Darkness falls…
…Still… I… am… Here…
…Holding back the lambent passage…

…Thump…

…Breathing fails…

…Stay away from the light…
…I… DEFY… YOU…
…Be gone… I fear thee not…

… …

…Free of the flesh…

…Time is the enemy…
…Flesh, its weapon of irony…
…It strikes me down…
Yet…

…STILL… I… RISE…

…

The Eve of Battle...

For now we stand
on the eve of battle,
beheld in the
growing shadows
of eternal darkness,
we are baptised
in a river of blood
beneath a sky of fury,
united as the fires of Hell
rain down
from the Heavens...

And our enemies
wait at the gates,
baying for our flesh,
craving our souls
that we may become
the meat puppets
of madness
as death heralds
the advent
of our corpses
rising to fight
among their number,
finding our place
amidst an army
of the dead...

We may not return,
we may never again
look upon the world
we once knew
through mortal eyes,
but we will be victorious,
for in honour and glory
shall we find release,
our fears screaming
to rage
as we hold aloft
the sword of truth
and bring the fight
to the hordes
of Abaddon's fury…

For in our hearts and in our souls
we know without doubt…

…TODAY IS A GOOD DAY TO DIE…

The Sentinel...

As the planets align
and darkness falls
over the Earth,
so will come
the dawn
of change,
a nexus point
where all that was,
is and will be
flutter on the wings
of anachronistic shadows
beheld in the eyes
of temporal flux...

An anomaly
of dormant potentials
that wait in the echoes
of the uncreated,
whispers of what
could be,
fighting
for existence
in a chorus
of dominion
that chant
in the impact
of shifting tomorrows...

For none can hear the cries
that shriek from the void,
growing in number,
growing in strength,
devouring
the causal nexus
in delphian nightmares
that fade before
the rising dawn,
leaving such
bitter uncertainties
in the supernova souls
of the dreamer's perceptions…

And so as the veil falls,
all shall see what awaits,
all shall know
what is to come
and all shall
see as I do,
but alas they rise
from the depths,
grafting
consciousness
onto a reality
that repels them,
yet weakens
to their onslaught
in the breach
between moments…

Time is running out,
for who shall
watch the watchers
when perception
is blind
and certainty
holds falsehoods,
crushed in the
hand of fate,
distorting as realities
converge
and merge
in the wake
of the
forgotten genesis…

I grow so very weary,
for so long
have I held back
the darkness,
a sentinel
to the entropy
that grows in the
fractured emptiness
of eternity,
holding back
the atrophy
of a world
whose time
should have
ended so very long ago…

Please tell me, I am not the only one…

A Postcard from the Edge...

Hi all,

Just dropping you a line to let you know we got here
okay... There seems to be some sort of hippy jamboree
going on to celebrate the Summer Solstice... They seem
like a wacky bunch but they know how to have a good
time... But a quick word to the wise, if they offer you
smokes or mushroom based drinks, in hindsight it's
probably better to decline... After a night of marinating in a
deck chair, smoking a huge doobie, discussing vegetable
politics with Captain Herbal Life and Gandalf the Green
over a pot of mushroom tea, I soon found myself tripping
my f**king head off, curled up in a ball with a cucumber
up my arse, begging for my life at the feet of the Lentil
Queen and her Potato minions... Not quite sure what
exactly followed but needless to say, I awoke to find
myself married to a badger called Derek... Apparently, it
was a lovely ceremony, although not my proudest hour...

I hope this card finds you well...

See you soon, lots of love,

Fritz.............

xxx

Fritz & Friends…
(Collaborative Works)

The following chapter features collaborative works Fritz has written with fellow poets across the world via online friendships, including **'Speak to Me (A Chorus of Voices)'**, a collaboration he orchestrated & edited that features 40 poets in one piece…

Poets in one on one collaborations include:

Fire Crystal…………........(New York, USA)
Janice Arndt……………......(Florida, USA)
Elizabeth Anne Winter……(Kansas, USA)
Margaret Boon…...(Bulawayo, Zimbabwe)
Lilly Wolf……………………….(Germany)
Leesey Smuland Clark………....(VA, USA)
James Owens……………........(Missouri, USA)
Kelly L.B……………........(New York, USA)
Avery Jones…………………...(Texas, USA)
Helen Dunn…....……………(Yorkshire, UK)
Becky Blake………………..(Yorkshire, UK)

Fritz & Fire Crystal...

The first piece in this collection 'The Princess, the Monkey & the Frog' is a metaphorical, fairytale, dedication piece in tribute to our daughters, Kali & Romana who each battle with Autism and strive daily to understand & interact with the world around them...

For Kali & Romana, with much love,
Fire & Fritz.....
xxx

The Princess, the Monkey & the Frog...

Once upon a time...
In a land not so very far away,
lived a pretty young
princess named Kali...
She was a loving child,
adored by all around her.
Her mother,
the great Fire Queen,
watched over her
with great love and affection...

But alas, poor sweet Princess Kali
had been cursed without speech
by the wicked Witch 'Autismo'
who had bespelled her
when the Fire Queen had banished
the ogre called 'Jerk'
who plagued her kingdom...
Little did she know that the ogre
had been the Autismo's son
and coveted her vast Kingdom...

She had sought help from Lexie,
Queen of the North
to overcome this great curse
and free Princess Kali...
And so with their combined strength
and vast armies
they set to seek out
Autismo the Witch...

Princess Kali,
meanwhile had slipped out
of the castle,
she walked swiftly,
quietly through
the beautiful forest.
Lost to her own thoughts,
humming a gentle tune to herself.
For though she spoke no words,
she was blessed with the gift of music…

Behind her followed
her two dearest friends.
A monkey that this fair,
young Princess called Boo
and behind him
a frog named Ribbit,
these two dear friends
knew the little Princess's
wishes and dreams…

This monkey and this frog
to others were simply stuffed animals,
to the princess
they were her dearest friends.
The only friends who understood her.
Through many adventures
they had already helped her
overcome so many obstacles
and in light of recent events,
they were called upon
to help her through many more…

Little did they know
as they walked along the forest path,
that other worldly forces
were at work against them.
Forces they would need
more fight and courage
than ever before to oppose...
They had unwittingly
wandered from the path
and into Dell of ticks,
beside the obsessive streams
and before long, night fell,
so they huddled up close...

Trying to stay warm
as the cold of night
started to seep in,
Princess Kali began shivering,
restless in a light sleep,
so Boo first cuddled under her arm,
trying to keep the chill
and the fear away
from the sweet Princess,
Ribbit heard a noise
coming from beyond the Dell,
so he listened carefully...

Voices approaching,
footsteps getting closer,
he recognised the voice...
It was Jerk the ogre
chasing fairies through the Dell
and all too soon,
he realized,
they had stumbled
into Autismo's domain...
Fearfully, he crept back to the Princess,
he did not wish to wake her,
nor could he leave her in sight
of the approaching ogre...
He had to think quickly...

Ribbit and Boo struggled to figure out
how to hide the princess,
they would have to awaken her.
They had to act fast...
Hastily, they shook the princess awake.
Startled by them,
Princess Kali jumped up,
they quickly shushed her,
alerting her that they had
stumbled into Autismo's territory
and Jerk was getting
ever closer as his footsteps got louder...

They slowly crept backwards
out of the dell,
trying to avoid capture
by Jerk the ogre...
But it was too late,
Boo had accidently
stood on a twig,
cracking it loudly
beneath his foot...

The Ogre stopped
and looked directly at them,
smiling gleefully
at the joy that this
would bring his Mother...
They tried to run
but were grabbed
by the branches
of the surrounding trees...

Struggling to break free
from the grasp
of the animated trees
proved to be harder
than they had hoped,
for though the sweet Princess
was very strong
she still could not
free herself from the tangle
of branches that held her...

Jerk the ogre started to creep
closer to his captives
when a scorching flame
suddenly shot
through the dell,
singeing the few hairs
on the ogres head...

The Princess's face lit up
with a big grin,
realizing that her mother,
the great Fire Queen
had found her...
Boo & Ribbit danced with joy
and the ogre roared and charged
as the Fire Queen came into view
through the charred trees...
She stood, unmoved as the ogre ranted,
foaming at the mouth in his charge...
Suddenly, when he was nearly upon her,
a sharp whistle shrieked through the trees,
throwing the ogre off his balance
as Lexie, Queen of the North
appeared beside him...
'You're mine' she said
drawing her magic sword
as the ogre fell flat on his face...

Queen Lexie laughed with delight
as the ogre writhed and wriggled
against her magic,
The Fire Queen freed
her beautiful princess
and dear friends from the trees.
She wrapped them all up
in a big hug while tears
flowed from her eyes...
Princess Kali smiled up
at her loving mother's face
with the brightest smile
you ever did see...

A sorrowed screech pierces
the air as Autismo strides
into the Dell to see Jerk
writhing beneath Queen Lexie's magic.
Too late to block,
Queen Lexie is thrown off her feet as
Autismo casts a spell at her.
The Fire Queen throws
flame after flame at her,
but she casts them aside
like they are nothing
and quickly overcomes her...

Princess Kali takes a hand mirror
from her pocket and runs
into the affray and holds it up to Autismo.
Magic is reflected back at her
and catching her reflection,
she is drawn into its gaze,
unable to look away as she is
dragged beyond the glass
to her reflective prison…

Trapped and screaming,
Autismo holds no power
any longer over
the pretty young Princess Kali.
She is free of her hold
but alas, not completely free of her spell,
for although still without speech,
she becomes the one
with the power over Autismo
and each day as she looks
deep into the mirror,
she knows her battle
would stay with her
for the rest of her life...

The Fire Queen
and Lexie, Queen of the North
merged their mighty kingdoms
that their fair and just rule
may hold favour over all their loyal
subjects as far as the eye could see,
beloved in their majesty...

And they all lived happily ever after...

Dark Reflections...

I see thine evil
through hollowed eyes,
it reflects mine own,
born of beautiful sin,
primal in the fires
of creation...

This torture tears
from within
blackening my heart,
hardening my dark soul,
strangled screams
can't escape,
silenced in a blanket
of darkness,
intoxicated
of sinister essence,
slithering serpentine lies,
embracing evil
to my open mind,
feeling so
very, very good...

My blood runs cold,
ice flowing
through my veins,
causing me to pant
through stitched lips,
lost to the lust
of my pain...

Choking on reality,
smothered
by blood red anger,
seething
in a pool of rage,
entwined
in all I become,
shaking off
the shackles
of murky past,
becoming
the demon within...

Deadly calm
creeping up
my spine,
harvesting evil
in my brain,
feasting on
the darkness within,
rising my demon
in sublime yearning
of deeds so grim
yet so fulfilling,
that it flows
like a river
of crimson intent...

Unraveled...

Thunder rolls
in a storm of rage,
another betrayal
that CUTS like a knife

I CHOKE on all
I want to say
as I TRY to breathe
through the PAIN,
the STENCH of lies
hangs thick
in the air
around me,
poisoning my SOUL
in the bitterness
of deception
and falsehoods

Her TRUTH,
a thinly
disguised veil
I clung to
for sanctuary,
BLINDED in the face
of ficticious adulation
that leaves me NAUGHT
but sorrow, anger
and heartbreak

Worry NOT,
I know of your woes
all to well,
but YOU my dear,
will live,
you will breath,
You will go on
and a BIG lesson
has been learned
this day.

I so wanted
to believe in you,
I so wanted
to love you
I so wanted
to be with you,
and you vowed
that...

...YOU...
would LOVE me...
...FOREVER...

Yet you
cast me aside
like petal torn rose,
USED, spent,
purpose served.

Cast out,
an angel falling
through a toxic sky,
LOST to despair,
mourning the love
of a...
...STRANGER...
who was not
who she claimed.
I shall KNOW better
next time...

Beware the TRICKSTER!!!

For NOW I go back
to barely existing,
wading through
a river of tears,
NUMB to
a stream
of LIES,
trying to...

...BREATHE...
without
air,
sinking
to
DEPTHS
of the
abyss
in an
ocean
of woe

...CLINGING...
to
a
thread
of...
...SANITY...
...as
the
tapestry
unravels...

Strings... CUT...
Puppet... FALLS...
...Tangled...
...Lifeless...

...BROKEN...

Arrogance Be Thy Name...

Such gifted Gods are we,
worshiped, nay plagued
by mortal adulation,
as they taunt us
with their petty grievances,
worship our greatness, yet...
they are not fit to hold our pens,
nor harbor our sadistic thoughts...

We weave the sickening webs
that bind the tapestry
of their meek, pitiful little lives,
we bring forth meaning
to their drab mundane existence...

We scribe our daily gospels
for the devoted minions
as they eagerly lap up every word
desperate in their envy
to emulate our passions,
trying to acquire
but an ounce of our gift
in their meager offerings...

But alas, it is beyond
their limited understanding,
too far above their comprehension
to appease their mortal hearts...

And so they must settle,
feast upon such tiny morsels
that we should see fit
to bestow upon them,
lusting all the while for more,
craving but a taste
of the greatness
we imbue upon the world...

And so they writhe and slither
like the worms they are,
yearning to earn our affections,
longing to bask in our love...

Behold us, for we are glorious,
bathed in the light of magnificence,
ascending to the mantle of Gods,
for we are the true creators...

...Bow down before us peasants...
...Kneel before your Gods...

For we are the mighty ones,
we sit upon the thrones
of divine literature...

Your ruthless Queen o' Fire,
beautiful to behold,
heartful to the soul,
vengeful of the infidels...

Your mighty King Fritz O'Skennick,
Lord of darkness,
bringer of chaos,
keeper of madness...

For we are here to feed you,
give you this day
your daily bread...
That you may feed
on the souls
of our labors...

So come one, come all
embrace the insanity
bestowed unto thee this day,
relish our words,
devour our divine rhapsody,
consummate our verse…

Behold us… Worship us…

…LOVE US…

Passions Cold...

Beholden to eternity's hand,
stood on the edge of forever
Lost and confused
in this world so cruel,
forsaken by my lovers eyes,
adrift amidst past mistakes,
drowning in an ocean of despair,
my body flanked in your anger,
hidden behind a quaint smile
that shadows the fear in my eyes,
beckoning a darkness that
numbs me to my core...

I wrap my arms around myself,
trying to block out the chill,
hating myself for my weakness,
ever craving your touch,
I can't deny this hunger,
my body screams with lust,
so primal in this longing,
such passion in my heart,
such desire in my soul,
for only your touch will do,
no other shall ever redeem you...

But alas, our time has passed
and so I lie, an empty, hollow shell
of potential's loss...

Fritz & Janice Arndt...

"Sheol's Wrath"

A blanket of night
shrouds a
patchwork landscape
of effervescent thoughts,
masking mortality,
hiding empty gestures
where deceptions
thrive and play,
igniting the
spark of rage
that burns to fury
in the flames
of purification
My demon rises
in a blaze
of blind acrimony,
tearing the gates
of Hell asunder,
beckoning the call
to the decievers,
taunting, waiting,
salivating,
relishing the
prescient whispers
that bestow
such lucid desires,
to strip their souls bare...

Gut wrenching
in its fervency,
intoxicating
in its ferocity,
devouring
mournful cries
of forbearance
and absolution,
enticing my
demon's appetite
watching, waiting,
shaking
as fear usurps
satisfaction,
crushing conceit
and audacity
to humility
and shame...
My horseman
ascend the beyond
amidst the souls
of the lost,
locusts to the storm,
tainting the world
in the scorpion's wrath,
poisoned in the
serpent's bite
as venom corrupts
the macrocosm,
quelling the innocence
in a flood of hypocrisies...

For I am Sovereign
to the Abyss,
standing on
the threshold
of Purgatory's hand,
luring darkened hearts
to Gehenna's inferno
who shall forever
seek an end
that eludes them...
Acrid smoke billows
amidst the
discontented cries
as torments
reek and rise
in a roar of
crackling flesh,
charred, flayed, raw,
eternally burning
on an
amaranthine pyre,
heads cast,
weeping, crying,
praying to a God
forsaken by them
in mortality,
as Horns sound
in triumph
as they choke
on the ashes
of defeat and damnation...

For who shall watch the watchers...

Hearts of Fire...

Hold me my love
and let thy fires burn,
and let thy passions rage
in a storm of lust.

Fan now the embers
of desire to flame
and ignite thine ardor.

Fevered hands tearing
at bound attire,
fingertips eagerly exploring
soft, sizzling flesh,
lips locked, tongues tied.

Arousing my senses,
consuming my mind,
unchaining
my deepest desires.

Fulfilling my thirst
with thy sultry juices,
drenching my hunger
as thou dost tremble
and quake 'neath my touch.

Thy lustful scent,
musky in its bouquet,
illuminates and intoxicates
in its own divine opalescent zest,
building my craving to burst,
driving my hunger for thee.

Nymphomaniacal night
bequeath me
her carnal tendencies,
lost to my opiate dreams
before me in flesh.

Such tumultuous
dark seeded yearnings,
evocative of my avidity,
soaring my hysteria
to climatic heights.

Dizzy, focused,
fading inhibitions
saturates thy
velveteen skin.

Tantalizing firstly
and most tenderly,
exploring, teasing,
taunting nipples
playfully without
stymie or constraint.

Soul laid bare,
stripped, waiting, wanting,
yearning for thy smooth,
silken touch.

Hands caressing,
stroking parted thighs,
immerse, become, submerge.
So softly beheld
the beckoning call
of that which awaits thee

'My Love, as thou dost softly whisper,
thy gallant words bring unto me
a frenzied fever, as like I know not,
breathless, panting, lustful
beyond my constraint or control.

So bold yet so gentle,
thy body calls to me,
arouses me, awakens me.

Vibrant to my womanhood,
I kneel before thee,
silently, longingly,
I dost become obedient
of thy command,
for this night,
this hour, this moment...

My knight owns me completely,
I give myself unto thee,
I betroth my love unto thee,
I am for thee as thou wouldst desire,
thy wish be my command...
Spake thy gentle words, my lord...

What wouldst thou hath me do?'

Life, Love and Fate...

Its hard to see the silver line
when clouds are black and gray,
and when it rains it really pours
my luck is bad today
but I know my rainbow lies
beyond the darkness here
because I dream and live to write
in words so soft and clear...

I'm building worlds inside my head,
from thoughts within my mind
creating words that bare my soul
and so my heart's defined
tomorrow is another day,
another bitter pill
but none can take my words from me,
the dreams I can fulfil...

The Silver line is there you see
when shadows pass our way
The rain is slowing down right now
the rainbow's here to stay.
Because we dream and live to write
our minds can venture out
the words replace the sadness now
the sun will shine no doubt...

Life is full of ups and downs
we face upon our path
the only way we can know love
is know the devil's wrath
for without hate, we'd know not love
we'd know no right from wrong,
the secret is the balance found
to know where we belong...

Sometimes balance hides from us
and makes life look so bleak
But even so our love must grow
to ever reach its peak.
To never love or take the chance
or seek what you desire
Would be so tragic in its loss,
like ice without its fire...

Cry Havoc...

And so be it,
the lines are drawn
this day,
the enemy,
stoking the fires
of war,
fanning the flames
of chaos
in their lies,
slandering our names
in propagandas,
bringing rage and hate
to raise an army
but we will not fear, no,
we will not bow nor bend
for we hold aloft
the banner of truth
that they would depose
without thought
nor conscience...

For each man knows
that the morrow
may never come,
that the sun
may never again rise
to their eyes,
children weep
as women grasp
their men in fear
that it be
their last embrace,
for if it truly be
their last embrace,
then they will know
the bitter taste
of injustice,
lost in a world
of falsehoods
that shall
never again
recover its maxim...

For in honour
of the fallen,
we shall rise
and call upon
our brothers
and sisters in arms
to fight for the memory
and the glory
of the slain
that their deaths
be not in vain,
as children walk
this bloodied path,
trained for battle
as babies of war,
innocence lost
in the blood
of most unholy deception,
that they should bare arms
and defend their
beloved kith and kin
as Mothers and sisters
lay abused
and savagely raped...

No longer will man
lead our war
nor run our countries,
for as the silence falls,
staying the dogs of war,
it will be
the war of wars
where women
scorned by battle and loss
shall pay any cost to survive
at the aggressor's mercy
and will feign to bow
to their beckoning,
plotting their reckoning
in a blow to drive
the enemy
from our shores...

The call of freedom
rings out
with clarity
throughout a world
of hope and belief,
a cry
from the Earth
'Enough is enough'
a whisper
on the ocean breeze,
a shriek
from the elements,
a rage
from the lands,
the call
of the innocent
as all we hold dear
lies in ruins,
democracy gone
as tattered flags
rattle
on brutal winds,
torn down
and burned
for warmth
and defiance
in the face
of betrayal
and a sense
of hopeless waste...

Yet alas,
across vast seas,
traversing oceans,
over a planetary pond,
our comrads come,
by ships of steel,
so shall
the cannons fire
as missiles
seek targets,
and the decievers fall,
so shall the tears
of hope rain down
in question
of all that
has gone before
'Could this
truly be
our salvation?'
The not so
United Nations
that has once again
turned it's back
on us
in a betrayal
of promised peace...

we must stand together
for if we lose
our comrads lose,
united albeit
for but a day,
a fresh hope,
an answered prayer,
washed anew
in the glow
of the righteous,
a power in numbers
as Karma steps in
with our brothers
a world away,
fighting
for what is right...

For on this day
we are not two countries,
we are not two sides,
we are people,
sharing a dream
of truth, justice
and freedom,
trying to save
our legacies
and salvage our lands,
trying to hold on
to our heritage
and human rights
and civil liberties
that all are equal
and justice is served
as bestowed to us
by the earth
and history's gift
as the word
of our forefathers...

...We shall prevail...

Fritz & Elizabeth Anne Winter…

(contains adult content…)

Seeping through the cracks in sanity...

I wake beyond a veil of truth,
such clarity in my illusions
with a sun that shines
in the dark of night,
lighting the coffee-stain shadows
on a quaking ground
beheld in the red rimmed eyes,
collapsing in a supernova soul...

I grasp for air with fevered hands,
fingers raw in the fading dusk,
tenuous footing losing ground,
balancing between
the darkness and the light,
slipping through cracks
in sanity to despair...

Slowly I plummet,
falling through hopes and dreams
lost on a failing path,
broken to the deceits
of fading yesterdays,
taunting my thoughts,
breaking me down as I crawl
through the gelid depths,
drowning in an ocean of lies
that quickly pass
in the shadows of truth...

Wisps of tomorrow
seeping through
the shattered
remnants of today,
dragging me under,
pulling at my tired,
flailing limbs,
chanting falsities
and empty promises
in equal abundance,
echoing to my cries...

'...No more... Please...'

One Dark Night...

Temples pounding through fingertips,
Demons clawing beneath my skin,
screaming to get out...

Intense rage burning through my mind
screeching to force understanding
of the beast that writhes within...

Such fury as he shreds my thoughts,
rewriting the world around me,
crashing the walls built to hold him...

Struggling against an overbearing tide,
wailing through clenched teeth,
grinding for strength to wage this war...

He glares through my red-rimmed eyes,
raw vocal chords quiver deeply
as he growls to speak my voice...

He roars from below the surface
Let me out... Let me live...
Control... I need control... Give me life...

Suppress the Demon... Quell his lies...
He shall not prevail, he cannot win,
he feeds my illusions, builds my hope...

Constructing sublime falsities,
peripheral to perceptions of reality,
setting me up to fall...

Feverish desperation, grasping solitude,
veins throbbing through tendon strained hands,
holding on to MY reality, not HIS... MINE...

One foot on the precipice of the void,
a maelstrom of shifting thoughts,
disipating in chaos to an army of voices...

Resounding above the storm, enveloping the darkness,
my voice booms, repetitive in its clarity...
MY voice... MINE... MINE... MINE...

Lost in the shadows of a fragmented mind,
embracing the shards of quintessence,
my bleeding soul concieves a growing anxiety...

...Am I the Demon I fear?

Caveo, malum of orbis terrarum es solvo

Precious the treasure, avails not my muse,
this verboten gift bestowed by great Zeus?
Tempt not devotion to pious decree!
Bequeathed enticement be pawn to thy ruse?

Beholdeth the beauty, mine gift from thee.
For sooth, be thy secrets that calleth me.
Its lust doth devour my dreams 'til I wake
O, by the gods, now begone! do I plea!

Forgive me, O' Zeus, thy wish I forsake.
Mine sapphire eyes so bespelled they doth break.
Mystery sated through carious glance.
Such glory beseech my heart to partake.

Dark evil bleeds through mine eyes so entrance.
The price be too steep, greed stabs like a lance.
Recoil in surprise, the vessel bound tight.
In hopes thou wouldst spare me, I beg perchance.

O Zeus, unto thee, mine eyes see the light.
In battle, my will, too weak to give fight
Twixt knowing or not, 'twas glimpse I didst choose.
Tho' once I stood proud, now shame is my plight.

Written in the Persian form of 'an Interlocking Rubáiyát' in an Olde English narrative with a Latin title, inspired by a Greek tale (Pandora's Box) and written by a Welshman & an American...
Multi-cultural enough for ya? LMAO!!!

Lament of the Damned...

Fermenting in the blight
of vagary, as I wallow
in excrement of futility,
and wretched misery enshrouds,
I lapse to an odious wail...
this lament of the damned
that tears my soul asunder...

Alas this hollowed shell,
home to my fading elan vital,
a means to traverse
the intricacies
of a cold sterile world,
so cruel in its neglect,
so lost on its path...

So unjust in its condemnations,
a harsh unsighted reason,
where standing only provides
a treacherous fall
into the depths of despair,
forever falling,
pulled on the currents
of sorrow in an ocean of woe,
can't breathe, blind,
lost in an all consuming darkness
that numbs the flesh
in its pervading kiss...

Burning Passions...

Beyond the depths of aching hearts,
a yearning in my soul
desperately desires burn
in flames from ember's coal

Passions rage yet holding back
anticipate the need
a breath, a touch, a tender sigh
as passion tempts to feed

Brushing lips as stirring grows
be still my beating heart
tensions rise at lust restrained
can't bare to be apart

Boldly tearing at our clothes
caress what lies within
a fevered grasp with ragged breath
my hands upon your skin

Inhibitions fading fast
I hold you closer still
impassioned lips feast hungrily
as need fulfills its will

Flesh so soft beneath my palms
our thoughts become as one
time withdraws as bodies meet
discard our doubts to none

I lay you down and taste of you
you gasp at tender touch
sight recedes as passions burn
want you so very much

Rising up to taste your lips
flesh glows a wanton blush
enter to a world of dreams
and gasp to feel its rush

a primal feast of starving hearts
results in merging souls
become as one beheld in lust
and make each other whole

Passion at Moonlight Lake

The stars shimmered,
casting an enchanting blue hue
upon the clear moonlit surface,
broken only by the soft ripples
as she floated weightlessly
without shame or inhibition...
A clear night sky whispered
with the barest hint
of a breeze
rustling through the trees...
The only sound,
the soft hum of water at her ears
Such freedom,
as she stroked the soft water
without restraint,
playful, calm, beautiful...

He glided beneath the surface,
his legs flexing
to the gentle under current
that brushed past his naked body,
soothingly as her bare flesh
was revealed
to his blurry water filled eyes...
He swiftly slowed his ascent
and smiled in anticipation
of her surprise
as he stealthily
eased up behind her

She tingled as the sensation
of water washed over her,
circling her breasts,
gently caressing
her shapely torso,
stroking and surging
between her legs,
causing her to coyly smile,
reminded of the smooth
caress of a man
with a tender embrace,
a longing caress
she quickly loses herself to,
a longing caress like a lover's kiss....

Oh how she longed for that touch,
the adoration of a man
who would love her without question,
would need her without doubt,
would want her with such undying passion
and make her feel like a woman...
She frowned and pondered for a moment
'No... She ached for the affection,
the attention, the hot passion of a man
that would not make her feel like a woman
but make her know she was a woman,
not just his devotion or his love...
She ached for his body...'

She gasped in surprise
as she felt his strong touch
upon her calves
and ease gently up her body,
past her thighs, over her hips
to snake around her waist
as he surfaced behind her
and gently kissed her neck...
She shivered and smiled,
moving her head to the side
as she reached behind her
to feel his firm hips and strong thighs...

Shoulder deep in the warm wash,
he sighed longingly
at her submission to his attentions
drinking in her beauty
so wanton to his touch.
Her hair, floating in the water as her hands
gently brushed against his thighs,
her soft touch sent his passion raging
from soft ember to burning flame...

He ground his teeth and clenched his jaw
desperately fighting to restrain himself...
"A little longer, hold off just a little longer...
Dear God in heaven, I want her so badly"
His eyes traced a floating lock
as he lightly grasped
this water maiden closer to him,
close enough that she would feel the fire
stirring in him as he stood tautly behind her...
Tenderly, he traced his finger along her shoulder,
her awareness of his intentions gladly met
in the desire in her eyes...

His movement had stirred
her awareness to new heights,
her eyes widened lustily
and she gasped to feel his ready passion
pressed against her...
She gasped again as he firmly turned her to face him,
gazing at her with such fire in his eyes...
Strangely, she did not fear him,
nor did she wish him away,
she quivered and caught her breath
as she felt passions pain in her loin
at the very sight of him...
She sighed and pondered for a moment
"If this is a dream, do not wake me,
let this dream take me."

His mind raced in his want of her
"Those lips... I must taste of those lips"
He pulled her to him once more,
dipping his head to satisfy his need.
She grasped him, her fingertips exploring
the skin of his neck, shoulders and back,
his mouth to hers in a ravenous frenzy...
He straightened, her body mirroring his action,
buoyed by the water to rest against him,
flesh against beautiful flesh.

In a moment, reason was blinded to her passion,
lifting her legs to embrace his waist,
a joyous shudder racing through her blood
as she felt his manhood pressing
and gently parting her...
She cried out and groaned
as he entered her,
the sounds of the night
become the sounds
of all consuming passion,
lusty moans punctuated by pleasure
and unrepentant need...

Fritz & Margaret Boon...

Slumber's Toil...

Insomnia,
an unwelcome visitor
in my home,
though sometimes
the barricade holds,
he still slips
through the gaps
of my waking mind,
feasting
upon slumbers hold
with obsessive thoughts
that shroud my weary,
red rimmed eyes.
Soon the light of a new day
will filter through the fatigue,
causing me to groan
and clutch my temples.
Reddened orbs weary,
sightlessly locked in
yesterday's fading essence,
demons clawing their way back
to the surface
as spectres
of time and memory.
Haunted in perception's
twilight grasp, lost
to the rising dawn
of decadent tomorrows
and entropy of life...

Please... Leave me to my torpidity....

Spellbound...

Alas this night,
yon stars doth fall
from velvety skies,
behold thee,
yonder words
dost spake,
reveal to me
thy soul for sooth,
perchance to dream
my true loves name,
for he who doth
call'eth me,
my love...

Alone in a crowd

Like lambs to the slaughter,
they follow the flock...
Like stinking, thieving magpies,
they're drawn to the shiny...

All the same, no contrast,
no independent thought...

Am I being cynical? No, I think not...
My life shall not be clouded
by rigid conformity...
My soul shall not be blighted
by the petty concerns of fools...

I shall seek to unfurl my internal vision,
push the boundaries of my imagination...
Shed light on that which
I perceive to be truth...
Ever vigilant to traverse
uncharted paths that lie ahead...

Paths that lie hidden beyond
the periphery of my mind's eye...
Thoughts that lie beyond
the perceptions of physical reality...

I shall wield my sword of truth
cutting through all the falsehoods that
fester and spawn through the void,
lurking behind pale sightless eyes...
I vouch that I shall live a blessed life...
I vouch that each night,
before slumber blissfully consumes
tumbled thoughts of waking mind,
I will reconcile the days events,
judge my actions as I would another...
Knowing beyond the sanctity of maxim,
that I have done my utmost
to live a true and decent life
and therein I will find my peace
and purity of mind and soul...

...One day at a time...

Rainbow of Delight

Double rainbows dance
a celestial ballet
upon silken clouds,
displaying vivid spectrums
of colour splashed hues,
touching through mists of time
bespelling joy of our magic union...

Raindrops falling, rainbow's calling,
caressing divine sensations
in a multicoloured fusion
of love's future path
walking hand in hand,
soul to soul
by eternity's touch,
fulfilling destinies,
so carefully beheld
in fragile hearts...

Fritz & Lilly Wolf...

To Eternity & Beyond...

Your heart it slowly seems to die,
your soul is hurting deep.
Drowning in the fear and lies,
that wake me from my sleep.

You should have stopped as you still could,
but now it's all too late.
Your end is near and so you stood,
embracing all your hate.

Like flowing blood it gave you life,
but now you cannot breathe.
It cuts me like a sharpened knife,
that you no longer sheathe.

And so you feel you'll end it now,
I'd like to hold you back.
But I really don't know how,
without the strength I lack.

I watch you fall but you are gone,
and now I long for you.
Your hurtful games went on and on,
my love for you was true.

Can you feel my breaking heart?
In death we can be one.
And nevermore be torn apart,
beneath the dying sun.

Fritz & Leesey Smuland Clark...

Loving You...

I love you so much...
So extremely, so deeply,
so macho, moocho, muchly...
A thousand, billion,
trillion, bazillion times
as many atoms and molecules
make up your body,
and as many grains of sand
that fill all the deserts
and all the beaches
In all the world,
ever created,
designed and made...
With as much depth
in as much water
that fills all the oceans,
rivers, lakes, ponds, creeks
and seas ever created
and rained down on the Earth
and evaporated
back up to Heaven
and back down
to Earth and back
to Heaven again
and again and again...
With a hugely ginormous passion
that transcends time, space, thought,
logic, life, death, paradox,
reality and eternity
with ten million, billion, killion,

catrillion, agillion, extremely,
extra intensely mega, huge gigantic
ginormous, giganta, humungous,
Jurassic, Godzilla, mammoth,
extra, extreme hugs and kisses,
my dear, dearest, sweet, sweetest
loving bundle of joy
who I adore more than life,
chocolate, alcohol and drugs!!!!!!!!!!
Coz you just make me feel
high on life and love
as I hold you in my arms,
thinking I'm so lucky
to have you in my life,
loving me as much as I love you!!!!!!!
This is the upper, upper,
over, over, champagne super-nova,
extreme, extreme lasting love
that never dies…
And its all for you!!!!!!!!!
XOXOXOXOXOXOXOXOXOXOXOXOXOXOXOX
OXOXOXOXOXOXOXOXOXOXOXOXOX
OXOXOXOXOXOXOXOXOXOXOXO
XOXOXOXOXOXOXOXOXO
XOXOXOXOXOXOXO
XOXOXOXOXOXOXO
XOXOXOXOXO
XOXOX
OXOXO

And guess what?
I luv ya…

Fritz & James Owens...

Beyond the Veil of Axiom...

Searching for the truth beyond
the lies of building terror,
cut from paths of blind deceit
that shows a world in error...

Born to lives of self beguile,
so pestilent our time,
empathy retired to dreams
bored child with barbarous chime...

Awaiting through the ages gone
when past is dust and bone,
exhaled upon the winds of time,
beyond the lives we've known...

For we must look beyond the glass,
beyond the surface veil,
to find the truth that lies beneath
in dreams as lies avail...

Facing truth of who we are
to find who we should be,
potential is the strength we seek,
bestowed to you and me...

But the quest is camouflaged,
their minds build up such walls,
illusions of virility,
the holy grail that calls...

The journey's end is drawing near,
the secrets hide the veil,
but the men who hold the power,
use fear on such a scale...

The puppet masters forfeit pawns,
enthralled by lavish ruse,
convincing us there's nothing there,
that all we'll try we'll lose...

The ones that hear the voices call,
that hide in minds of woe,
the madness in the eyes of some
that longs to let us know...

To tell us what's beyond the veil,
to warn what we must do,
to add to knowledge long amassed,
in lives we never knew...

So behold the coming storm,
accept of this our fate,
the walls will fall in shifting veil
as darkness lies in wait...

Time is ticking slowly on,
the candle snuffs its flame,
shadows fill the lives we knew
and whispers call our name...

So beware the end of days
and heed the voices calls
as all we are just fades away,
devoured as darkness falls...

Fritz & Avery Jones...

The Devil's Lullaby...

My heart is dark,
but the night is darker...
Where is my soul?
Lost to the demon's song,
a meat puppet,
waltzing to a mournful lullaby,
that turns my heart to ice...

Strings cut...
Falling...
Forever falling,
craving an end
that never comes...

Torn... Caught twixt
passion and loathing,
thrashing my bloodied flesh
in penance of my damnation...
My soul exposed to darkness,
with little left to breathe
of its sweet, intoxicating effusion,
blanketing me in its essence...
Devouring me of my mind...

So strong... So very strong...
Voices calling,
enticing me,
swooning me to sway
to the Devil's lullaby,
to serenade a dark desire
in a symphony of despair...

My soul devoured,
making me watch
your every deviance,
making me crave
my mortality's end,
from your torment
through my hands...

A hollow man
stripped of purpose,
consumed by madness,
decaying in the entropy
of a broken mind...

Help me....

Fritz & Kelly L.B.

Dead Inside...

Seeking clarity
in a world of illusions,
wrapped in a blanket of lies
look around, what do you see?
Deceit flowing into a crimson steam
forever spilling through the cracks in reality...

Demons rage in the shards of falsities,
emerging in hordes,
waiting to attack,
feeding on a
broken mind,
beheld pleadingly
by searching eyes
that bleed despair...

Tear stained eyelids
Recoil from light,
shown through windows
in her mind,
painting such
sorrowful thoughts,
numbing her
to the core...
She sobs,
realising
she's dead inside...

...Speak to Me...

The following poem is a collaboration of 40 poets from all over the world as orchestrated by Fritz O'Skennick... It began on the poetry site: Allpoetry.com in the group 'Speak to Me' as the group were invited to contribute lines on the topic board in a form of poetry tag/Chinese whispers then seamlessly edited to a singular narrative by Fritz...

The following is a credit list of all the poets involved in the making of this piece:

Fritz O'Skennick (Wales)......................Lyrikel/Kelly Elmore (USA)
Tony Goodwin (England).............................knightcall/T.L. (USA)
Pyrozia/Claire Liebmann (USA)...............Loving-Dove/Maggie (USA)
SheWolfNLust/Debbie Altiparmakis (USA)...................Montey (UK)
SoulSpeak/Elizabeth Anne Winter (USA).............Sportay/keith (USA)
Holly Golightly/Denise Mason (USA)...................Joseph Alan (USA)
CherryOnTop/Janice Arndt (USA).................A63-Angel/Patsy (USA)
Sharon Marie/Sharon Lagueux (USA)..................pebblesbaby (USA)
Debbysmiles/Debby Sorensen (USA)............Elizabeth Grace II (USA)
Viyanna Rosemarie Langager (USA)...............Poetic-Theorem (USA)
GoddessofSensuality/D.A. Baugh (USA)
Laura0757/Laura Spizzirri (Canada)
afireinthisheart/David Eisenberger (USA)...Paladin Warrior/Joe (USA)
Joey The Poet/Joey Wilson (USA)....Soulful Woman/Noreen Agis (USA)
LittleSoulSister/Caitlin (USA).................Aries/Kath Piels (Australia)
SoulfulBubbles/Kassandra K (USA)....Mystic-Fire/Jenny Jordan (USA)
Nevel/Erwin Kroon (Netherlands)............brerae1/BreAnna Rae (USA)
Glasyalabolas/Brian Hosie (Scotland)
Deepness within/Jayne Dale (Wales)
PurpleKnickers/Deborah Jane Samson (UK)
rhymanshu/Himanshu (India)...............jayray1975/marc j. ray (USA)
crimsondew/Firdous Arjumand (India)
BluesMan/ William J. Reed IV (USA)

Speak To Me (A Chorus of Voices)

Prescient whispers bestowing gifts of eventide,
seeking divine pardon and retribution…
Fore there, from the silence,
stares the face of the lonely,
an echo of beauty that glimpses
of a forgotten past,
a face, a shadow of romance,
falling from the stars,
trailing the dust of the heavens
beneath the gentle moonbeams glow,
blue in the crescent joy that smiles upon us…

Your hand brushes mine and fingers interlock
as if to mock the tragic sorrow
that racks our inner beings,
beheld as the hand of darkness holds us fast,
bestowing memories that no one
could ever erase,
dreams that will never fade
as our loving force braves the stormy weather.
The very stars align, stranger still as I catch them
as each hold our fate like fiery streamers of light,
waiting to break free;
journeying our hearts forward,
passed the shadows of foreboding fear…

We are brilliant, we are incredulous,
we embody the eloquence that speaks
through love's secret unfolding,
learning to face all fears,
time moving us forward to embrace
whatever lies ahead…

Facing those fears bravely with courage and vigor,
for if nobody makes a stand today,
we will lose an opportunity to make things happen
in the face of new beginnings...
And that will be our downfall, our loss...

So one by one shall we stand together
with the divinity to do and say what is right.
Unite in confidence so that our voices
may be heard in chorus,
that we may sing the sweet sounds of victory
in forgetting the past injustices
of those that trespass against us.
Moving us forward into new tomorrows,
bathed under beautiful skies
as we sit beneath trees of weeping willows,
branches gently swaying to remind us
of our fading yesterdays...

Yet they tease our perceptions
with a sweet, silent promise
of tomorrow's dreams...
And so I sit by the water, staring into my reflection,
my love staring back at me, locked in a lovers' gaze,
sand between our toes,
with only the moon bearing witness
to the union of our shadows,
growing ever longer in the shifting light,
for something special is happening
as we watch the stars fall from the sky,
shooting stars, bestowing hopes,
as we make our wish come true...

Behold our dreams bleed into reality,
a moment in time that changes our world
in the blinking of an eye
You, I, the world will never be the same,
for we embody the emotions of the universe,
uniting lovers with our bridge of happiness,
leaving footprints in the sands of time,
a path of the journey we are on.
Shifting the tide of dreams
that gently streams
with the current of a nearby river,
moving the sands under our feet,
spellbound in the beauty of the horizon afar,
warmth felt as hearts touch…

Softly the sounds of birds chirp a lullaby,
surrounding us in their sweet
and tender song.
If we can but allow ourselves
to feel that freedom,
embrace that joy, let go of the woes
that bind us to the sins of the past
and so reclaim our lost innocence
and in wonderment
so many voices will sing as one;
sweet as honeyed wine.
In unison, we will sing joy;
through the trees to all that was
all that is and all that will be…

Fore we, the dreamers, duty bound
to share our graceful song
with a world of compassionate dormancy.
For the others are awaiting our call,
locked away for reasons
that God only knows,
prisoners of injustice,
prisoners of circumstance,
prisoners of persecution,
prisoners of their own minds...
But we are as one with the Universe,
reaching to the heavens for the stars,
so that we may let all unfold
and be as it should be,
that we may find peace with our God...

Beneath the folds of the ocean's sweeping kimono,
hides a little girl as brown as unstirred tea,
softly she whispers the grace of the universe
under the pale, white noh mask
of a beautiful woman.
A silent breath of grace embodied
as sweet innocence shines on the noh face...
A gentle breeze stirs the jet black tresses
as she moves with the grace of a ballerina,
elegant in her posture,
refined in her stature,
divine in her humanity,
a vision of hope beheld
in the dreams of tomorrow...

Reflections of comet's kismet happenstance
move across her eyes, her eyelashes misty,
her breath subdued as she ponders love
and how it will come to pass
in her own lifetime,
as the nightshades of her eyes
slowly imprison her to her dreams,
ethereal visions of lovers dancing
on the silent breeze of a star filled sky…
…And she is so entranced by these moments…
Moments that only live within her,
embracing her fevered heart, clinging tightly
to bring home this magic that awakens
from so deep within her,
to become a yearning she must sate…
Where the sprinkling of stars
bestow silvered wishes
that hover and glide
with a wraith like beauty,
that bespells her heart in its longing
as the sweet morning sun
casts its healing rays
over her sleeping countenance…
A simple melody plays along
with her chimera footfalls…

He glances behind him,
his eyes full of such sorrow and regret,
tears that meander on virginal paper,
searching for the words to fill
the emptiness of his soul,
basked under a sleepy, twilight sky,
which knows beyond
the unspoken thoughts
why the wind still blows
and the dawn still rises
to embrace a new day
in the cycle of eternal balance
between the darkness and the light…

Yet such fleeting ink as words once spoken,
still hang in the air like spider-silk,
intricately weaving his questions,
as delicate as a gentle whisper
over and under and again…
"what might have been?"
and more pointedly, he whispers a sigh
as gently as the softest kiss
a mother could bestow
upon her beloved infants brow…
"what could be?"

Is this world worthy of our souls meander?
She is so very desperately in love
and so she ponders the thoughts
of what true love really is...
In her minds eye, she sees fluffy sheep
playfully bouncing in a lush meadow,
a metaphor of innocence
wrapped in a cotton candy dream
as her essence of childhood
mingles in a whirlwind of whispers,
desperately calling out to those
with the strength to seek the same…

Such dreams that find birth in the shadows;
and from the depths of inner darkness,
creativity and imagination are born,
that we may scribe the voice's doctrine,
beyond the demon's grasp,
etch our thoughts in the truth of our souls,
behold our pain and our desires
bleeding our axiom on an empty page,
that others may know our hearts...
Yet, she knows of no solemn scorn
but holds that which is dear
and clutches it tightly to her breast…
For what was once her heart,
so full of happiness and bliss
now becomes threatened by the fear
of darkness lingering in the still umbrage…

But the ray of hope still remains
and by sheer will alone,
she carves out that hope
from the pervading shadows,
held high, the light within the darkness…
Her faith, her purity, her wonderment,
driving back doubt
in its spell of brightness,
leaving but one question
lingering upon her soft lips
"What are you waiting for?
Just cast it and see the magic grow"

And so today, a gleam of light,
burns from the passion of a true heart
and plays on the walls,
creating dancing shadows,
dipped in the ink of fresh hope
to quill the dreams that for so long
were chained within,
as the shadows lay in wait
to change what fate
her heart truly desires…
And as the darkness slowly draws near,
she cries out for her lover's light
to cast the shadows from her sight…
He turns, heeding her cries of desperation
and so the light of day
eclipses his silhouette,
brushing warmth upon her face
but alas to no avail,
and seeing no change
in her co-dependant hell.
He gently whispers…

"For too long, have you stood in my shadow,
draining my life to enrich your own...
Step into the light and save us both
before the wellspring of love runs dry."

All she can do
is quickly nod with happiness...
She smiles and takes his hand,
boldly leading them
out of the darkness
and into the light
to hear a chorus of voices
who dare to scribe their tale
in unity and strength...

We are the hearts, we are the souls,
we are many, we are one voice,
we are the thread
that sows the tapestry of life...

...Speak to me...

Fritz, Becky Blake & Helen Dunn …

CHAV 101: Know Your Enemy!!!

Chav life:
Great Britain On the Fritz...

by Dr Fritz O'Skennick

Chavs are quite easy to spot on the streets of Great Britain...

Clothes
Chavs generally tend to be bound by the traditions of their tribes in the manner of their dress... Name brand trainers, tracksuit bottoms & a hoodie top are generally accepted amidst the tribes. The baseball cap is a lesser commodity donned by their young and worn through adolescence and by some into adulthood... Its marks a right of passage and acceptance in its familiarity to other clan members... All manner of dress will cost a small fortune, displaying status in their customary mating rituals. Each item of clothing comes with a label demonstrating its authenticity and are liked particularly for the bright shiny colours as opposed to written inscriptions, for alas they have yet to evolve a written language. Meanings to words such as Adidas, Umbro and Rebok have yet to be deciphered by tribe elders...

Appearance

Dead eyes, brown, broken or missing teeth, shaved heads and large chimp like ears combined with a hominid brow that gives them their almost ape like appearance largely unseen since the extinction of Neanderthal man... Much of this is attributed to inbreeding due to the knowledge that nobody on their housing estates are really outside of the family...

Bling

Chavs generally adorn themselves in all manner of talismans & decorative jewellery. From large gold rings that perform a secondary function as a knuckle-duster, for ongoing battles with their enemies, the police... Ear rings & neck chains that give them the appearance of white trash, A-Team rejects of the Mr T fan club ensure copulation in their customary mating rituals...

Language

Chavs generally communicate in a series of grunts that are widely understood by the tribe at large. Although they have been known to mimic odd words and phrases in an attempt to communicate with the larger populace in a slurred lazy manner that enforces the belief of primitive culture... "Oi, lend us a fag, dont be tight." "You queer or what?" or "Where can I score some weed?" are typically mimicked phrases in their attempts to communicate. But one must ensure that should you have to respond, you use words that are less than 3 syllables lest the chav becomes confused and quite often aggressive in the belief that you are disrespecting his status and deliberately antagonising him...

Personal Hygiene

Chavs have no sense or knowledge of the term, to use it would infringe the less than 3 syllable caution and incur their wrath (see appendix 4). It is the belief of the tribe, that washing, cleaning teeth or even bathing are time consuming or to use their vernacular "Fuck That!!!" (A term fully embraced by the tribe at large)... Quite often, they try unsuccessfully to mask that scent of stale body odour by spraying vast quantities of de-odorant about their bodies. But no amount of sweet smelling potions stand a chance in masking an odour that has been decades in the making. It is also believed amongst the tribes that to wash ones hands after visiting the toilet is a sign of weakness and incurs homosexual behaviour. Those among them who have managed to grasp a basic concept of written language assume signs above urinals that state 'Now please wash your hands' are an amusing punchline to entertain while they relieve themselves and sinks and hand dryers are just ornamentation to brighten the drabness.

Now that you know what to look for let us delve deeper in to the culture that spawns them...

Clan Beliefs

The concept of working for a living is deemed offensive to the Clans at large, they believe that the country's workforce is primarily in place to pay taxes in order to finance their drug and alcohol needs and house them in a manner befitting their status within the tribe. Any wants not met are quickly stolen from those who have them, their logic deriving from the belief that why should you work for it when you can steal it? To the Chav, a job is a fool's game that pays for those who do not wish to work.

Child rearing is based on a concept of life experience, largely regarded by the public as a form of neglect, whereby the child is had mainly for the extra income that can be claimed upon its birth and the house that will be given to the mother. At age 5, said child will be roaming the streets between the hours of 4pm-11:30pm, allowing its parents the liberty of drunken escapades in the belief that the child will learn the ways of the world through its experience in the gangs formed on the housing estate where they dwell. (for further information refer to the section on 'Chavlings')

Hunting Grounds

From Barry Island in Wales to Scarborough in Yorkshire, you'll find Chavs in their hundreds swarming Seaside tourist spots, lots of shops selling cheap, tacky merchandise and T-shirts, lots of chippies and penny arcades galore. Why they ascend these spots in the Summer months largely remains a mystery, but most studies believe it is another mimicking gesture, in that they believe they are holidaying. Further study is needed, but infiltration remains an enigma when dealing with loud yobbish families who communicate in grunts. Easily spotted, they roam in packs, spreading chaos and bad dress sense wherever they go. And so grunt-speak becomes the county dialect. If caught in such a place during the Summer months, refrain from asking 'Could you speak in English please? I don't speak Grunt...' (see appendix 4) It has long been held in belief that these said tourist spots have been targeted for Military strike as a last resort should their numbers become too large for the economy to deal with, so ending the credit crunch and the drain on society, manners and the living standards of decent ordinary people...

Mating Rituals

The mating call of the male Chav is believed to have been derived from discourteous builder's speak... Calls of "Get your tits out" "Suck this Bitch" and "I'd fuck the arse off you" have long swooned the female Chav and so begins the mating courtship, whereby the male will take a territorial stance, fighting off any potential rivals to his chosen female that day. He then performs many daring feats of driving, including, wheel spins, ridiculous speeds in populated areas & reckless endangerment of life with loud, booming, bass and drum tribal music emanating from the car... Excited by this, the female quickly presents her assets to the male, lifting her top or bending over to show the thong that has been wedged between the cheeks of her backside since last Summer and texting sex grunt to the male... The female can breed with up to 40 males during any given Summer in the belief that the strongest male will dominate the essence of her offspring quickly procreating ASBO the next generation... Many Chavs who procur an emotional attachment to a chosen mate develop what can only be described as the rudimentary basis of a relationship. Occasionally mistaken as human as they walk among us, bystanders have often been shocked at their tender displays of affection. To the male, nothing says I love you like a punch in the face, (part of the mating ritual), quite often mistaken for violence, people have tried to intervene in the belief that they are helping the female from this violent onslaught by the male, only for the female to attack them, perceiving them as a threat...

Chavlings

The offspring of the Chav quickly learn the ways of the tribe... Destruction of property, stealing and fighting are all embraced by age 5. After many run-ins with their mortal enemy, the Police, by age 15 they have a keen knowledge of the law that could give the best lawyer a run for his money. It is a proud day for the young chavling when he is bestowed his first court order ankle bracelet, displaying to other tribe members he has begun his ascension to adulthood. He will strut around the streets of the housing estate with great pride, blatantly defying his curfew order, furthering the qualification of the inevitable ASBO that will follow... A proud day indeed...

Chav Olympics

Every year Chavs gather in populated town and city areas for their annual Olympics ceremony. Festivities generally begin with an all out riot at the local football stadium at the height of the season with an epic battle (on the scale of Lord of the Rings) with the riot police. Points are given for originality of weapon choice based on what they find around them, although most just bring their own, with the winners judged on the trophies procured from the enemy, ie: police helmet, truncheon, radio and bonus runner up prizes for the looter's spoils...

Now that the games are underway and the competitors are warmed up, it bleeds into the street and is perceived by the public at large as a senseless crime wave of mindless proportions. Although, it is interesting to note that the games officially begin in the ceremony of the burning cars as torched by last year's gold medallion winners. A police car is big points to the lucky Chav daring enough to pursue it... And so the games are officially under way... Firstly comes the drug test and any contestants found to be not taking any are quickly disqualified from events.

Events include shop window shot-putt, wheel hub discus, tag looting, mortal combat and DVD relay, after all what better way to make a Chav run faster, than to tuck a DVD player under his arm. The festivities finally end after a night of untold chaos, countless arrests and millions of pounds worth of damage… With local news coverage resembling publicity shots and trailers from 'Planet of the Apes'

You can generally recognise the remnants of the night's festivities trolling the streets in the early hours by their manner and appearance. These include an aggressive, total invasion of personal space to anyone they meet, complete loss of inhibition and language skills, loss of bladder control and prone to waking up battered and bruised in a dumpster with amnesia & their car keys up their backsides, swearing blind that they have had the most amazing night ever...

Cultural Impact

There is much in media creation that can be attributed to inspiration of Chav culture. For example, in computer games, we find 'Grand theft auto' that is an almost direct representation of a Chav in a city centre but lacks authenticity in that it grants them a modicum of intelligence. Another game that adds a surreal take on the drunk Chavs in the city scenario is 'Resident Evil' which depicts brain-dead zombies whom the player must battle to escape said city before a military strike levels it to the ground. Often believed to be a simulation of previously mentioned Military Strike (see section on Hunting Grounds). And of course not forgetting 'Sonic the Hedgehog' after all, there is nothing the Chav likes better than collecting Gold rings.

What can be done?

As Chav infestations remain on the increase throughout the cities and towns of Great Britain, much is being done in scientific circles to counter the disruption this causes to the population. It is feared that such infestation could eventually lead to assimilation and devolution, leading to a Chav state of lawlessness, ignorance and low intelligence, throwing cultural advances back thousands of years to a simpler time of barbarianism and tribe mentality. Professor Becky Blake of Scarborough University has hypothesised the creation of an expensive range of sportswear that would appeal to Chav's sense of attire and perceptual stimuli. Said sportswear would be lined with memory metal filaments that when exposed to electro-magnetic fields could slow violent reaction, accompanied by electrically charged jewellery based on the principle of shock collars that could help with behavioural modifications in the Chav. Thus bringing riots to a quick and peaceful resolution with the police armed with no more than electro-magnetic plates lining roads and streets that when activated stop the Chavs in their tracks. Such sportswear would be labelled with target patches embroidered to hoodies, baseball caps and tops to ensure marksmen have a clear shot of more troublesome Chavs that are able to avoid the influence of the electro-magnetic plates. Although in the preliminary stages, prototypes have proved effective in the first stages of testing.

Professor Becky Blake 'Fuck em, the Chavs are a menace'

In conclusion, society largely remains powerless to act against an aggressor that has no sense of value, decency, moral fibre, law, loyalty, friendship or courtesy to others. And until, government addresses this growing problem, decent ordinary people will be forced to live in fear and outrage while the Chav culture thrives in its onslaught of the **NOT** so United Kingdom.

Fritz & Helen Dunn...

Arr... Bum-Hug... (A Christmas Rant)

It's Christmas Eve and all is still,
A time of peace and love's goodwill...
Good King Wenceslas, Silent night,
Time for men to see the light...
All is quiet through the house,
Nothing stirs, not even mouse...
And why?

Because I squished the little bastard when he took out my
TV cable. As if I haven't got enough frigging problems
without some fuzzy-faced, whisker-twitching rodent
destroying the one thing that gets me through the farce and
fake cheer of consumer spending and manipulation...

And talking of fuzzy-faced, whisker-twitching rodents,
does anyone else find the thought of some fat, beardy,
weirdo, who has you under surveillance all year, breaking
into your home and leaving gifts, the slightest bit
disturbing? This is what we tell our kids, it's no wonder so
many of us end up in therapy as adults... 'Come sit on
Santa's knee, little boy, if you've been good, you will get a
big surprise...' Fuck Me! It's the stuff of nightmares...

And we leave out cookies & sherry for him. I mean... What
kind of example are we setting? An obese, borderline
alcoholic who's partial to sugary treats and works one day a
year! Get your gin soaked whiskers out of the cookie jar
and get on a treadmill, you fat fucker... Anyone else would
be in danger of keeling over or arrested & breathalysed for
piloting a flight bound vehicle under the influence... Trust
me, there's only one fat, greedy bastard who's happy to put
gifts under your tree and his name ain't Santa, you call him

your bank manager…

Then there's the stroll round the shops soaking up the festive atmosphere, almost like a Dickensian scene, munching a mince pie here and a glass of mulled wine there as the Salvation Army gently serenade us with 'Silent Night'… LIKE FUCK!!! Violent Fight more like… Trying to get to the other side of the street is like threading a frigging needle. Crushed in the heavy throng of people as you prepare to do the WWF smack down so that you get the very last limited edition 'Barbie Sparkle Princess' which they neglect to tell you is only actually limited edition until January the 1st, then mass produced in the thousands.

So then, three cracked ribs and a black eye later you stagger up to the cashier, holding aloft your spoils of war, expecting the 'How may I help you?' and 'Merry Christmas' but instead he glares at you like you've just stirred his coffee with your penis… You'll be lucky if you get a grunt out of the miserable C**t!!! Then to add insult to injury, he opts to answer the phone instead of serving you… I mean, all I actually did was make the effort to get to the store and queue for hours on end, while some lazy, bone-idle wanker sits at home in his under-ware scratching his arse and getting first class service… Christmas shopping!!! HA, I'd rather stick my nose up Bernard Mathews' arse and have him fart poultry up my nostrils…

I mean, don't get me wrong, I'm not totally Bah Humbug but I could kick Tiny Tim's crutches out from under him & drop kick the little fucker into an electric fan... I mean WTF? Christmas carols in shops in October? Let me enjoy Halloween first, Please!!! Its much more fun... Don't let the do-gooding, smiley, Sally-Anne, trumpet blowing, money-grabbing, guilt-laying bastards take it away from me... Please!!!

And how do we prepare? Crying over credit card statements 'cause our kids create Christmas lists that run the length of 'War and Peace'... Cleaning the house in preparation for the big day, to the tune of 'I want this' and 'Get me that' after every advert?

And the tradition of placing the fairy on top of the tree was probably created by some poor sod who'd had a guts full and performed a pine-scented endoscopy on his wife who just happened to be playing Tinkerbell in the local Panto...

Then there's the wrapping of the presents, we lovingly spend hours wrapping gifts, with paper that should quite frankly be gold-plated for what it costs. A little fold here, a bit of tape there and big shiny bow on top for good measure... Then we step back and take pride in our handiwork as we arrange them just so under the tree... And for what? To watch the little bastards rip it all apart in under a minute?

Then there's the Queen's speech, the highlight of British television on Christmas day, highly anticipated, nudge nudge, wink wink... more like, a badger wrapped in a curtain with a sparkly plant pot on her head, wearing a look on her face like someone's waving a turd under her nose. And get this, she's trying to tell me she understands how hard I've got it from her fully staffed palace and countless millions she sleeps comfortably on. Really not feeling her sincerity...

And what is it we're celebrating? I mean don't get me wrong, loving the nativity scene, three guys, a woman, her husband and a donkey... No hang on, that was a nasty film I caught on cable the other night...

But how do we celebrate? We buy a turkey that looks like its mother got fucked by an ostrich...
Yes, the Christmas dinner!!! Hours spent peeling, boiling, roasting and cooking in the bleak hope it will resemble the Yule Tide treat as seen on TV (Thank you Jamie 'fucking' Oliver)... Timed to perfection, lost to the joy, pure poetry in motion... What a crock of shit... The reality, everything is timed wrong, sprouts are extra soggy, roasts are like bricks (which you later catch the kids throwing at the neighbour's cat) and the turkey is so dry and stringy you could knit a frigging jumper with it...

Then as the timing gets further and further behind everyone starts loitering around the kitchen like the cast of 'Oliver Twist' ready to fight the dog for any scraps... And no amount of 'Oom pa-pa' or 'Boom-titty-titty' is gonna make it cook any faster, so Fuck Off and consider yourself at home in some other poor fucker's house... And by the time this crap is served they are all so hungry and sozzled they would eat dog turds in wallpaper paste and swear it tastes like sausage and mash!!! And so commences the feast, as we pull crackers and wear paper hats, slowly getting pissed on wine and brandy as we all fart our brains out 'til the room smells like the toilet tent at Glastonbury. Thank you sprouts!!! What is it with the British and sprouts? Nobody else likes them! They don't even eat them in Brussels! Yet every Christmas, we fill our plates and live in fear of shitting our pants as the room fills with toxic gas that any other time of year would be considered an Act of

Terrorism. Who needs Anthrax when you have sprouts?

Then comes the biggest kick in the bollocks of the festive season, having had to take out a mortgage to pay for the fucking day, everything becomes half price and below the very next day…

And the people… All year round, they're rude, boorish, opportunistic pricks who'd pimp their own mothers for a couple of bucks… But flash them a bit of tinsel and few shiny lights and all is forgiven as they want to join hands and sing 'Auld Lang Syne'… Well Fuck You, You Asshole!!! You'll get my boot up your arse, 'cause you'll still be a prick next year…

And on that note I bid you

"HAPPY FUCKING CHRISTMAS!!!"

Luv,
Fritz & Pink….
XXX